6-14

**SCHOLASTIC**

# *Perfect Poetry Playlets*

Read-Aloud Reproducible Mini-Plays That Boost
All-Important Speaking and Fluency Skills
to Meet the Common Core

by Jacqueline Sweeney

NEW YORK • TORONTO • LONDON • AUCKLAND • SYDNEY
MEXICO CITY • NEW DELHI • HONG KONG • BUENOS AIRES

## Dedication

For my husband, Jim Quinn, and my friend, Peggy Hansen.
One hears the music in my head, the other the music in my heart. Love and "Kivem."

## Acknowledgments

Special thanks to editor and poet extraordinaire, Liza Charlesworth, and to dream editor for a writer and teacher, Dana Truby as well as to my agent and friend, Marian Reiner. And for all the TEACHERS who never waver from a deeper vision in education, who love the whole child and know that children are so much more than their test scores, an endless "Thank You" for all that you do.

Cover and Interior Designer: Holly Grundon
Illustrator: Holly Hannon

# Contents

# Foreword

*By Jacqueline Sweeney*

This book is for teachers who believe that poetry is essential in the elementary classroom. If you are reading this foreword, chances are YOU are one of them! Close reading of poetry can potentially transform students' relationship to the written word, as they discover the ways in which figurative language works and how each word plays an important part in the text. Beyond that, the performance of poetry provides children with the unique opportunity to learn how voice and expression contribute to a poem's meaning. In addition, students get the chance to boost fluency —and confidence—by reading aloud in a supportive, engaged environment.

I've spent my whole life teaching poetry and prose writing to children. As a teacher and artist-in-education, my practice has been to design language-arts lessons that build students' confidence—lessons in which even the most poetry-resistant students find themselves delighting in their own experiences as readers, reciters, and writers of poetry. I'd like to think that 40 years of practice has added up to something—a useful resource contained in this book that will help you give your students an authentic experience with poetry and save you time as a teacher. I hope that your students enjoy these poems as much as mine have over the years.

# How to Use This Book

This is truly a book for all seasons, with sixteen poems divided into four units, each tied to a seasonal theme. The poems are written expressly to match the interests and humor of kids in grades 3–5 and the needs of the classroom teacher. There is plenty of room to adapt the lessons, as savvy teachers do, to lower or higher grades.

Each chapter focuses on one poem and includes a "Teaching the Poem" section with suggestions on how to lead discussion, questions to ask your students to prompt deeper thinking, and extension activities. It also includes an illustrated Readers Theater reproducible play version of the poem to share with your students. These short reader's theater poem plays are a perfect bi-weekly addition to your language-arts curriculum. They will help ensure that your students have ample access to poetry and the rich and meaningful experience that is Readers Theater.

The strong seasonal and curriculum connections also make these poetry lessons easy to pull into your language-arts program periodically throughout the year. For example, the first poem is ideal for the first few weeks of school. In "Waiting for the Bus," an older boy who has his own mixed feelings about going back to school helps his little sister cope with her first day of kindergarten and her first ride on the bus. The poem is designed for ten readers and revels in the honking-bonking sounds of the yellow caterpillar bus as it rumbles and groans its way to and from school with our reticent elder sibling and hero on board.

Your students might also enjoy "The Dastardly In-Betweens," a poem designed for eight readers about a student stuck between two seasons and not knowing how to get out of one and into the other. Careful reading and deductive reasoning are required here!

Then there is the longer winter poem: "The Washington–Lincoln Chat." This Presidents' Day poem is anything but dull. It's filled with facts, embedded quotes, and interesting dialogue between the presidents. It is designed so that every member of your class can participate. It has two choruses and a group of drummers—perfect for those students who need to be active.

Of course there are shorter poems as well—little moments of observation that you can cover in a half-hour block, such as "Moon Poem" or "Choose a Color." And for those sports-minded kids there's "First Time at Third," which is an interesting study of embarrassing moments amidst fist-whomping, line-driving action on the field.

The summer section kicks off with "Who's in the Bog?" another poem that gets the entire class involved in performance. It features lessons in animal life cycles and metamorphosis with a polliwog, snake, and turtle hatchlings. It's a wonderful opportunity to make simple paper costumes and design a performance for younger students.

# Why Use Poems for Readers Theater?

Poetry emerged from the oral tradition and in most cases is meant to be read aloud, making it a perfect way to give students the opportunity to experiment with voice and expression. There's nothing like it to showcase the sound and sense of words and discover how meaning and feeling can be joined together in a powerful way. Reading poetry aloud helps stimulate students' thinking about poetry, hold their interest, and touch—as William Butler Yeats once said—"the deep heart's core."

Performing poetry plays helps reinforce the poetic techniques you are teaching your students such as alliteration, simile, metaphor, personification, strong verbs, word choice, point of view, and tone. Alliteration is far easier to understand when you say the words aloud, for example.

# Seven Steps to Successful Classroom Readers Theater

Readers Theater is a great way to enrich your students' reading practice and bring joy to your language arts class at the same time! Performing these poetry plays engages students and helps gets them excited about poetry, reading, and theater. At the same time, it builds valuable skills, increasing comprehension and fluency. Here's how to get started:

## 1. Model Expressive Reading

Once you've chosen a poem, start by reading it aloud to your class at least twice—once to engage their feelings and ears, once to engage their minds and eyes. Ideally, you should make copies for each student and project the play with an interactive whiteboard, document camera, or projector. Use your readings to model how expression, pace, and inflection help communicate meaning. For example, take a line from the poem and read it slowly and then quickly. Read it quietly and then loudly. Ask kids: How does the way we read a line affect it's meaning? Then, invite kids to read aloud with you.

## 2. Try Choral and Echo Reading

Choral and echo reading are great techniques for giving your students the confidence and practice they need before they read aloud on their own. It also helps build fluency. To do choral reading, you and your students read the entire poem together as a group. That way, all your students read at the same pace and with the same phrasing and intonation. In echo reading, you read a line and students then repeat it, echoing your expression, tone, and pacing.

## 3. Assign Roles

After you read the poem aloud as a class, have students take turns reading it aloud. If some of your students are reluctant to read aloud, assign two readers to each role. If you are using a document camera or projector, assign one student the role of "pointer." He or she can point to each line of dialogue in turn. If students have copies of the play, have them use highlighters to mark their lines. Give them time to read over their lines, before reading it aloud.

## 4. Teach the Laws of the Theater

Explain to your students that they need to speak loudly so that their voices can be heard easily. Encourage students not to worry about small mistakes. Tell them: Just ignore a slip up and keep going. If the audience laughs, pause until they stop and keep going. The show must go on!

## 5. Form Readers Theater Groups

After you've done a few poems as a whole class, consider breaking your class into groups and having them perform one of the shorter poems on their own. Encourage group members to work together and decide how they want to perform the poem. Together, they can experiment and explore the characters. What voices will they use? Will they make simple props? The different performances of the same poem will give students extra opportunities to observe Readers Theater techniques and to absorb the poem.

## 6. Share the Wealth

Consider having your students perform their Readers Theater for another class in the same grade or the grade below. Students could perform for parents at an event—or you might videotape the readings and share them online for families to enjoy.

## 7. Write Your Own Poem Plays

Once your students become truly comfortable with Readers Theater, challenge them to do their own poem-to-play adaptations. Have students work in pairs. Each pair can choose a well-known or student-written poem to perform for the class. What a great way to build community!

# Meeting the Common Core State Standards

The poetry lessons in this book meet the following Common Core Standards for grade 3–5 according to corestandards.org. (Specific Grade 4 standards are provided as examples).

## Comprehension and Collaboration

CCSS.ELA-Literacy.SL.4.1 Engage effectively in a range of collaborative discussions (one-on-one, in groups, and teacher-led) with diverse partners on grade 4 topics and texts, building on others' ideas and expressing their own clearly.

CCSS.ELA-Literacy.SL.4.1a Come to discussions prepared, having read or studied required material; explicitly draw on that preparation and other information known about the topic to explore ideas under discussion.

CCSS.ELA-Literacy.SL.4.1b Follow agreed-upon rules for discussions and carry out assigned roles.

CCSS.ELA-Literacy.SL.4.1c Pose and respond to specific questions to clarify or follow up on information, and make comments that contribute to the discussion and link to the remarks of others.

CCSS.ELA-Literacy.SL.4.1d Review the key ideas expressed and explain their own ideas and understanding in light of the discussion.

## Presentation of Knowledge and Ideas

CCSS.ELA-Literacy.SL.4.4 Report on a topic or text, tell a story, or recount an experience in an organized manner, using appropriate facts and relevant, descriptive details to support main ideas or themes; speak clearly at an understandable pace.

CCSS.ELA-Literacy.SL.4.5 Add audio recordings and visual displays to presentations when appropriate to enhance the development of main ideas or themes.

CCSS.ELA-Literacy.SL.4.6 Differentiate between contexts that call for formal English (e.g., presenting ideas) and situations where informal discourse is appropriate (e.g., small-group discussion); use formal English when appropriate to task and situation.

## Key Ideas and Details

CCSS.ELA-Literacy.RL.4.1 Refer to details and examples in a text when explaining what the text says explicitly and when drawing inferences from the text.

CCSS.ELA-Literacy.RL.4.2 Determine a theme of a story, drama, or poem from details in the text; summarize the text.

CCSS.ELA-Literacy.RL.4.3 Describe in depth a character, setting, or event in a story or drama, drawing on specific details in the text (e.g., a character's thoughts, words, or actions).

## Craft and Structure

CCSS.ELA-Literacy.RL.4.4 Determine the meaning of words and phrases as they are used in a text, including those that allude to significant characters found in mythology (e.g., Herculean).

CCSS.ELA-Literacy.RL.4.5 Explain major differences between poems, drama, and prose, and refer to the structural elements of poems (e.g., verse, rhythm, meter) and drama (e.g., casts of characters, settings, descriptions, dialogue, stage directions) when writing or speaking about a text.

CCSS.ELA-Literacy.RL.4.6 Compare and contrast the point of view from which different stories are narrated, including the difference between first- and third-person narrations.

## Integration of Knowledge and Ideas

CCSS.ELA-Literacy.RL.4.7 Make connections between the text of a story or drama and a visual or oral presentation of the text, identifying where each version reflects specific descriptions and directions in the text.

## Fluency

CCSS.ELA-Literacy.RF.4.4 Read with sufficient accuracy and fluency to support comprehension.

CCSS.ELA-Literacy.RF.4.4a Read grade-level text with purpose and understanding.

CCSS.ELA-Literacy.RF.4.4b Read grade-level prose and poetry orally with accuracy, appropriate rate, and expression on successive readings.

CCSS.ELA-Literacy.RF.4.4c Use context to confirm or self-correct word recognition and understanding, rereading as necessary.

# Reading Tips

Distribute copies of the poetry playlet to your students and have them spend time in small groups discussing the poem and practicing before you read the poem aloud as a group.

Readers 1–3 should set the initial, somber tone by reading slowly and carefully—pausing on the words "waiting... waiting... waiting."

Readers 4–6 can speed up ever so slightly as the tone begins to shift. Readers 5–6 should shiver and wiggle as they read aloud "and thoughts of school/just make me shake."

Readers 1–2 then return with rapid-fire speech. It's important that each group of readers practice together so that their words fire out with even rapidity.

Have all ten readers repeat the last line rhythmically as they move in tandem (like a big caterpillar bus) off the staging area and out of sight.

# How to Teach "Waiting for the Bus"

"Waiting for the Bus" is a tour-de-force poem that takes a nostalgic look back at summer as it celebrates the beginning of school. The setting? Waiting for the bus on the first day of school.

## Questions to ask students:

**1.** Is the speaker excited or nervous for school to start? Both? What evidence can you find in the poem?

**2.** Do you hear *alliteration* in this poem? Alliteration is the repetition of a sound at the beginning of two or more neighboring words. Examples: "book bags in bunches" and "blinking, bug-eyed bus bumping."

**3.** What is the *tone* of the poem—the mood that the author creates for the audience? Can students point to places in the poem where the tone shifts or changes?

**4.** Can you find examples of *onomatopoeia*? Onomatopoeia means using words whose sounds suggest their meaning. Examples: *snorting, rumbling, thumping, honking*.

**5.** Can you find examples of the poet's use of humor?

**6.** The bus is compared to both an insect and an animal. Can students find these comparisons in the poem?

## Extension Idea:

Write your own "first day" poems. It could be the first day of soccer season, the first day for a new baby, the first day of vacation, the first day of middle school. Brainstorm ideas together and then give your class some quiet writing time.

# Waiting for the Bus

*By Jacqueline Sweeney*

We're waiting for the bus,
the bug-eyed bus;
book bags in bunches,
lunches crunched.

First day of school
and we are waiting...
　　　waiting...
　　　　　waiting...
for that bug-eyed, caterpillar bus.

Yesterday was Labor Day:
one last hotdog on the grill,
one last sunset at the lake.

The air and I are turning cold,
and thoughts of school
just make me shake.

My little sister makes a fuss
'cause it's her first day on the bus,
the yellow, blinking, bug-eyed bus
that's bumping down our street.

I hold her kindergarten paw.
She makes believe we're barking dogs.
We growl and pant 'til she is calm
and sitting in her seat.

Our snorting bus sounds like a hog.
The driver watches in her mirror.
My sister's fine, but I'm a mess!
It happens every year.

My stomach flip-flops every fall
to see the friends I haven't seen,
to see who's changed—or still the same,
and which friends wave and shout my name!

Teachers—lockers
Sneakers—books
Questions—answers
coats on hooks,

sign-in sheets
new desks and chairs.
And each day
I must be prepared

to learn more than the day before.

I wonder if I will survive
a hundred and seventy-nine more!

Our bus number is finally called.
My kinder-sister's in her seat.
She holds my hand.
I hold her paw.

The bus is bumping towards our street.

Our rolling, snorting, rumbling,
thumping, homebound-honking bus.

This caterpillar-highway-ruler
takes good care of us!

If there's one thing we can count on
in both rain or sister-fuss,

it's our gas chugging, kid hugging
good old bug-eyed bus!

# Waiting for the Bus

*By Jacqueline Sweeney*

**PLAYERS:**   Readers 1–10

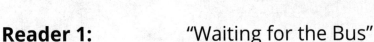

| | |
|---|---|
| **Reader 1:** | "Waiting for the Bus" by Jacqueline Sweeney |
| **Reader 1:** | We're waiting for the bus, the bug-eyed bus; |
| **Reader 2:** | book bags in bunches, lunches crunched. |
| **Reader 3:** | First day of school and we're waiting... |
| **Reader 2:** | waiting... |
| **Reader 1:** | waiting... |
| **Reader 3:** | waiting... |
| **Readers 1-2-3:** | for that bug-eyed, caterpillar bus. |
| **Reader 4:** | Yesterday was Labor Day: |
| **Reader 5:** | one last hotdog on the grill, |

**I → MORE**

**Reader 6:**   one last sunset at the lake.

**Reader 4:**   The air and I are turning cold,

**Readers 5 & 6:**   and thoughts of school
just make me shake.

**Reader 7:**   My little sister makes a fuss
'cause it's her first day on the bus,

**Reader 8:**   the yellow, blinking, bug-eyed bus
that's bumping down our street.

**Reader 7:**   I hold her kindergarten *paw.*

**Reader 8:**   She makes believe we're barking dogs.

**Readers 7 & 8:**   We growl and pant 'til she is calm
and sitting in her seat.

**Reader 9:**   Our snorting bus sounds like a hog.
The driver watches in her mirror.

**Reader 10:**   My sister's fine, but *I'm* a mess!
It happens every year.

**Reader 9:**   My stomach flip-flops every fall
to see the friends I haven't seen,

**Reader 10:**   to see who's changed—or still the same,

**Readers 9 & 10:**   and which friends wave and shout my name!

**Reader 1:**   Teachers—lockers

© 2014 Scholastic Inc. • *Perfect Poetry Playlets* • page 11

**Reader 2:**      Sneakers—books

**Reader 3:**      Questions—answers
**Readers 1-2-3:**      coats on hooks,

**Reader 4:**      sign-in sheets

**Reader 5:**      new desks and chairs.

**Readers 4-5-6:**      And each day I must be *prepared*

**Reader 6:**      to learn more than the day before.

**Readers 1-10:**      I wonder if I will survive
a hundred seventy-nine more!

**Reader 7:**      Our bus number is finally called.

**Reader 8:**      My kinder-sister's in her seat.

**Reader 7:**      She holds my hand.

**Reader 8:**      I hold her *paw*.

**Readers 7 & 8:**      The bus is bumping towards our street.

**Reader 9:**      Our rolling, snorting, rumbling, thumping,
homebound-honking bus.

**Reader 10:**      This caterpillar-highway-ruler
takes good care of us!

**Readers 9-10:**      If there's one thing we can count on
in both rain or sister-fuss,

**Readers 1-10:**      it's our gas chugging, kid hugging
good old bug-eyed bus!

3

## Reading Tips

Have your six readers stand in different spots in the staging area. As they say their first lines, each reader walks towards the center of the stage, reading loudly and clearly as they walk.

The readers will then stand together, bodies angled slightly towards one another, but mostly towards the audience.

The poem is short, so each reader should make the most of every word and phrase. Encourage students to read the first half of the poem with a child's voice. The second, adult-voiced part of the poem, should reflect a shift in tone— from exuberance to seriousness.

# How to Teach "Milkweed Time"

"Milkweed Time" is a memoir poem in which the speaker, as an adult, looks back at a yearly event: the end of summer. When the milkweed would pop out of its pods in late August and early September, it would float like silken parachutes and cover everything with a thick carpet of white softness.

## Questions to ask students:

**1.** What do we know about the speaker? Is it a child or a grownup? How do we know? Point out to your students that the poet chose to use the first person. Consider having students read the poem aloud substituting *he* or *she* for *I*. How does this change the tone or feeling of the poem?

**2.** Call students' attention to the shift in time from past to present that occurs in the fifth stanza: "Now when I see downy clouds...." Which word tells the reader that the narrator is no longer a child? Use this opportunity to reinforce the power of words in poetry. A single word can dramatically change both the time and meaning of an event.

**3.** Talk to students about *personification*. Personification is the act or technique of ascribing human attributes to nonhuman or inanimate things. Can students find examples in the poem (e.g.: "clouds hitchhiking" and "lumpy pods doing their jobs")? Challenge students to think of their own examples of personification, such as "flowers dancing" or "wind moaning."

**4.** Introduce the concept of *symbolism*. A symbol is something that represents something else, as a heart symbolizes love. Ask students: *What does milkweed symbolize in the poem?*

## Extension Idea:

Break your class into small groups and assign each group a different color or shade of a color. Ask the groups to brainstorm all the words, ideas, and emotions that might be associated with their color. For example, *blue: ocean, calm, sadness*, etc. Remind them to consider nature, history, geography, and literature as they compose their list. Have groups share their lists with the class. Use these lists as the jumping off point for color poems!

# Milkweed Time

*By Jacqueline Sweeney*

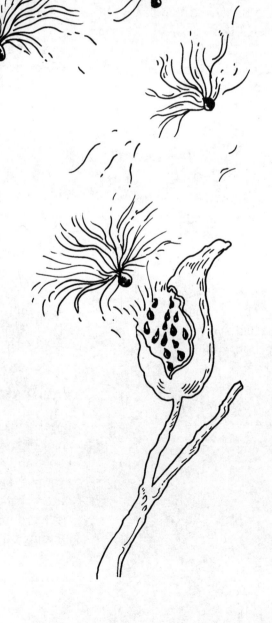

When I was small
I picked a brown and lumpy pod.
I thought it was a big cocoon.
But it was hard and dry and odd
and wouldn't hatch.

Instead one day
it cracked,

and out puffed gobs
of silken hair, clinging
to my hands and clothes and skin,
filling the meadow air
with strands

so much like kitten fur
I listened
for the purr.

Now when I see downy clouds
of parachutes
hitchhiking on
the early autumn wind

I know it's milkweed time
and all those lumpy pods
have done their jobs,
have scattered
all the roads and fields with
milkweed snow;

and I wish each time
that summer
didn't have to go.

# Milkweed Time

*By Jacqueline Sweeney*

**PLAYERS:**   Readers 1–6

**Reader 1:**       "Milkweed Time"
by Jacqueline Sweeney

**Reader 2:**       When I was small
I picked a brown and lumpy pod.

**Reader 3:**       I thought it was a big cocoon.
But it was hard and dry and odd
and wouldn't hatch.

**Reader 4:**       Instead one day
it cracked,

**Reader 5:**       and out puffed gobs
of silken hair,

**Reader 6:**       clinging
to my hands and clothes and skin,

**Readers 1, 2:**   filling the meadow air
with strands
so much like kitten fur
I listened for the purr.

**MORE** ➡

**Readers 3, 4:**   Now when I see downy clouds
of parachutes
hitchhiking
on the early autumn wind

**Readers 5, 6:**   I know it's milkweed time
and all those lumpy pods
have done their jobs,

**Reader 1:**   have scattered all the roads
and fields
with milkweed snow;

**Reader 2:**   and I wish *each* time
that summer
didn't have to go.

*Read simultaneously*

**Readers 1, 2, 3:**   I wish that summer.....
I wish that summer.....

**Readers 4, 5,6 :**   didn't have to go....
didn't have to go....

**All Readers:**   didn't have to go....
didn't have to go....

2

## Reading Tips

The "Between __ and __" sections should be read rhythmically and rapid-fire like a fast-paced game of Catch.

The "Goodbye" line should be read with exaggerated comic sorrow, and the "Hi" proclaimed with over-the-top excitement.

The two stanzas that contain the line "Fall must be here someplace" reveal the culminating meaning of the poem.

Be sure Reader 3 loudly enunciates "It's Indian Summer!" as this is the key phrase that explains the meaning.

The second to last stanza "Please help un-stick me" should be a tour-de-force of pleading. Tell your students to read it as if they were begging to stay up late!

# How to Teach "The Dastardly In-Betweens"

"The Dastardly In-Betweens" is about that nebulous time between the two distinct seasons: summer and winter. The narrator feels stuck between the two. And the reason? The weather. It feels like summer, yet acts like fall. The culprit? Indian Summer.

As you begin, explain that this poem offers word clues like small relics in a treasure hunt, pointing the way to the ultimate prize: The reason for the narrator's frustration at being stuck between two seasons.

## Questions to ask students:

**1.** What clues does the title offer us? What does the title tell us about the poem's tone? Tone is the writer's attitude toward the subject. A poem's tone may be playful, sad, angry, serious, etc.

**2.** Explore the seasonal themes in the poem by making a Summer/Winter chart on chart paper or your interactive whiteboard. Ask students to call out words and images associated with the seasons and list them on the chart.

**3.** Ask students if they understand why the speaker feels so stuck. You might ask your class to offer examples from their own lives when they too, have felt at odds because of "dastardly in-betweens." Perhaps on Sunday nights as the weekend comes to a close? Or the last days of a vacation?

## Extension Idea

Have your students work in groups. Either assign them or have them choose a month of the year. Then, invite your students to brainstorm things they love about their month—holidays, clothing, weather, food, sports, activities, family traditions and celebrations, etc. Each group can cut out pictures from magazines or print them from the Internet to make a collage of words and pictures that represent their month. When they are finished, hang your visual calendar in the classroom and use it as inspiration for monthly journaling or poetry assignments.

# The Dastardly In-Betweens!

*By Jacqueline Sweeney*

Between
Labor Day          and     Hannukah
maple green and     red
lemonade     and     pumpkin pie
summer swims     and     sleds

Between
centerfield     and superdome
crabgrass     and     snow
"Play Ball!"     and     "Fight! Fight! Fight!"

Where am I to go?

Something happens to my freedom.
Something happens to my head.
When late night drive-in-movies
are replaced by: "Time For Bed!"

Something happens to my thinking
when my fishing poles and sleep
are replaced by "Do Your Homework!"
and alarm clocks' dings and beeps.

Goodbye mowers— Hi, snowblowers.
Goodbye cookouts on the dock.
Goodbye rowboat, hello notebook
"fall behind"—and "Set That Clock!"

But what of the in-betweens—
the dastardly in-betweens?

Some people *WINTER* in Florida—
Some people *SUMMER* in France—
But where do you find them
when summer's behind them?
Where do they go when they *FALL*?

Do they fall into winter? Or fall into leaves?
Out of gezundheit? Or into a sneeze?
Do they fall out of tanktops and into long
sleeves?
What *DO* they do in between?

Between
skateboards   and     skiing   and
putters     and     pucks
Yankees     and     Steelers and
 Tigers     and     Ducks

          Between
pretzels     and     eggnog and
hammocks     and     beds
summer and winter
whirl 'round in my head!

Fall MUST be here someplace!
Dad just bought new rakes.
Mom's carving a pumpkin.
There's turkey to bake.

It's Indian Summer!
My breath blows NO FOG.
Fall MUST be here someplace
and I'm a **FALL HOG**!

So please help *un-stick* me.
Oh help me, oh *p-l-e-a-s-e,*
for I'm stuck in the middle of
**IN-BETWEENS!**

The Utterly Ghastly
and SO—Unfantastically
Dastardly In-Betweens!

# The Dastardly In-Betweens!

*By Jacqueline Sweeney*

PLAYERS:     Readers 1–8

**Reader 1:**     "The Dastardly In-Betweens!"
by Jacqueline Sweeney

**Reader 2:**     Between Labor Day and Hannukah

**Reader 3:**     maple green and red

**Reader 4:**     lemonade and pumpkin pie

**Reader 1:**     summer swims and sleds

**Reader 2:**     Between centerfield and superdome

**Reader 3:**     crabgrass and snow

**Reader 4:**     "Play Ball!" and "Fight! Fight! Fight!"

**Reader 1:**     Where am I go to?

**Reader 5:**     Something happens to my freedom.
Something happens to my head.

**Reader 6:**     When late night drive-in-movies
are replaced by: "Time For Bed!"

**I** ➡ **MORE**

**Reader 7:**    Something happens to my thinking
when my fishing poles and sleep

**Reader 8:**    are replaced by "Do Your Homework!"
and alarm clocks' dings and beeps.

**Reader 1:**    Goodbye mowers...

**Reader 2:**    Hi, snowblowers!

**Readers 1, 2:**    Goodbye cookouts on the dock

**Reader 3:**    Goodbye rowboat...

**Reader 4:**    hello notebook

**Readers 3, 4:**    "fall behind"—and "Set That Clock!"

**Readers 1, 2, 3, 4:**    But what of the in-betweens—
**(together)**    the dastardly in-betweens?

**Reader 5:**    Some people WINTER in Florida—

**Reader 6:**    Some people SUMMER in France—

**Reader 7:**    But where do you find them
when summer's behind them?

**Reader 8:**    Where do they go when they *FALL*?

**Reader 5:**    Do they fall into winter?
Or fall into leaves?

**Reader 6:**    Out of gezundheit?
Or into a sneeze?

**2**    **MORE** ➤

**Reader 7:**     Do they fall out of tanktops and into long sleeves?

**Reader 8:**     What *DO* they do in between?

**Reader 5:**     Between skateboards and skiing

**Reader 6:**     and putters and pucks

**Reader 7:**     Yankees and Steelers

**Reader 8:**     and Tigers and Ducks

**Reader 5:**     Between pretzels and eggnog

**Reader 6:**     and hammocks and beds

**Readers 5–8:**     summer and winter
whirl 'round in my head!

**Reader 1:**     Fall MUST be here someplace!
Dad just bought new rakes.

**Reader 2:**     Mom's carving a pumpkin.
There's turkey to bake.

**Reader 3:**     It's *INDIAN SUMMER*!
My breath blows NO FOG.

**Reader 4:**     Fall MUST be here someplace
and I'm a FALL HOG!

**Reader 5:**     So please help *un-stick* me.

**Reader 6:**     Oh help me, oh *p-l-e-a-s-e,*

**Readers 5, 6:**     for I'm stuck in the
middle of IN-BETWEENS!

**Reader 7:**     The Utterly Ghastly

**Reader 8:**     And SO—Unfantastically

**Reader 7, 8:**     Dastardly In-Betweens!

*(Readers 1–6 repeat the last three
lines together, followed by the entire
class chanting these lines until all
readers leave staging area.)*

## Reading Tips

The poem is read by five readers who tell the story in a straightforward manner.

The pace should accelerate with the lines: "He's practiced on spaghetti. He's practiced on...." The pace should slow down again with: "So here's that loop again, Shoe." Readers 4 and 5 might act out the shoe-tying attempt as they say these lines.

"It's done! It's done!" should be read with spirit—and "except for problem one," should be read slowly, emphasizing each word.

The ending may be played for laughs with Readers 1 and 2 popping out the questions: "His Thumb?" and "Not Done?" with a surprised tone.

The final line should be said with great mock sadness—punching out the word "can't."

# How to Teach "Little Brother's Shoelace Blues"

"Little Brother's Shoelace Blues" is pure fun. It is an observational poem in which the speaker, presumably a big sister or brother, watches little brother struggle with learning to tie his shoes.

## Questions to ask students:

**1.** Ask students: *Who is the speaker? What clues tell us?* See if students can tell you that the title gives us the answer.

**2.** Introduce the concept of *figurative language* to your students. A *simile* is a comparison of two dissimilar things using "like" or "as," whereas a *metaphor* is a comparison between dissimilar things that does not use "like" or "as." Point out the metaphors in the second stanza: "Shoelace holes are snake holes..." and "His bows are droopy butterflies..." Ask your class to turn these metaphors into similes. Do they notice a slight shift in meaning and rhyme?

**3.** Explore the poet's use of repetition in stanza three. What do these repeated lines tell us about the little boy who is the subject of the poem? Invite your students to think of a time when they have shown similar determination to master a new task.

**4.** The fourth stanza has a "how to" quality with its description of the step-by-step progression of shoe tying. Explain how the author's relating of each arduous step in the process shows the difficult nature of a task we often take for granted. Can students think of any other simple tasks that might be broken down into steps (e.g., writing in cursive, riding a bike, bouncing a basketball)?

## Extension Activity:

Ask students to recall a time when they were learning something new: how to whistle, how to swim, how to hit a baseball, etc. Then, have them write step-by-step instructions for doing their chosen task. Have students read each other's "how-tos" to see if they can follow the "step-by-steps!"

# Little Brother's Shoelace Blues

*By Jacqueline Sweeney*

He's tried and tried to tie you, Shoe.
He's never done it yet.
A loop that flip-flops on the floor
is as close as he can get.

Shoelace holes are snake holes
where laces always hide.
His bows are droopy butterflies
that always come untied.

He's practiced on spaghetti.
He's practiced on the mop.
He's practiced on his sister's hair
until she made him stop.

So here's that loop again, Shoe.
He holds it with his thumb.
He wraps the other end around
and yanks it into bows...

It's done!

It's done!

except for problem one:

Little brother
can't remove his thumb.

# Little Brother's Shoelace Blues

*By Jacqueline Sweeney*

**PLAYERS:**    Readers 1–5

**Reader 1:**    "Little Brother's Shoelace Blues"
by Jacqueline Sweeney

**Reader 1:**    He's tried and tried to tie you, Shoe.

**Reader 2:**    He's never done it yet.

**Reader 3:**    A loop that flip-flops on the floor
is as close as he can get.

**Reader 4:**    Shoelace holes are snake holes
where laces always hide.

**Reader 5:**    His bows are droopy butterflies
that always come untied.

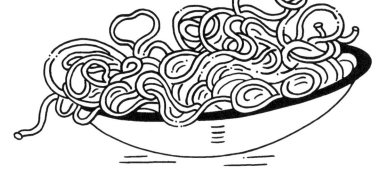

**I**       **MORE** ➡

**Reader 1:**      He's practiced on spaghetti.

**Reader 2:**      He's practiced on the mop.

**Reader 3:**      He's practiced on his sister's hair
until she made him stop.

**Reader 4:**      So here's that loop again, Shoe.
He holds it with his thumb.

**Reader 5:**      He wraps the other end around
and yanks it into bows...

**Reader 1:**      It's done!

**Reader 2:**      It's done!

**Reader 3:**      except for problem one:

**Readers 4, 5:**  Little brother
can't remove his thumb.

**Readers 1, 2:**  *(hands in the air)* His THUMB?

**Reader 3:**      *(nodding a big YES)* His THUMB.

**Reader 1, 2:**   Not Done?

**Reader 3:**      *(shakes head NO)* Not Done!

**Readers 4, 5:**  Little brother CAN'T remove his thumb.

## Reading Tips

Begin the poem at a normal pace. Have readers gradually speed up until the parts for Readers 5–8 are moving quickly.

Point out that words connected by hyphens should be read without a pause for breath, as with "sled-slides-and-spins."

Throughout the poem, the job of Readers 1–4 is to slow down the pace, and the job of Readers 5–8 is to speed it up again. So when readers 1–4 reappear with the line "But Tim is roof-zapping," they are putting on the brakes for words and phrases and meaning.

Readers 5–8 should keep the pace of the poem quick and lively, as if they were driving a sleigh with horses.

When all of the readers join the chorus for the final lines, allow them to repeat it joyfully as many times as they like.

# How to Teach "Winter's Assistants"

In "Winter's Assistants," the characters Caroline, Peter, Heather, and Tim are fanciful personifications of winter snow and sleet.

## Questions to ask students:

**1.** Introduce the concept of *personification*. Personification means ascribing human attributes to nonhuman or inanimate things. Ask students: *Who are the assistants? How are they assisting winter? What aspects of winter weather does each character represent?*

**2.** Point out the word *fandango*. A fandango is a lively Spanish dance involving castanets, guitar, swirling couples, and song. The music halts suddenly at certain points in the dance, and dancers freeze in place until the music begins again. Ask students: *What does the poet mean by a "winter fandango"? How does this dance style mimic the action of snow?*

**3.** Talk about the use of *onomatopoeia* in the poem. Onomatopoeia is the use of words whose sounds suggest their meaning.
 For example, the sound of the words "hush-a-hush…" emulates the sound of snow falling. "Hush" is also used in the poem as a command to silence the trees so they can listen to directions for the winter ballet.

**4.** Ask students to look for examples of *alliteration* (the repetition of the same initial consonant sound in neighboring words) such as: "snow-swirling," "foot-freezing," and "sled-slides-and-spins," or the flurry of repeated *w* sounds in the poem's last lines.

## Extension Activity:

Invite students to choose one of winter's assistants (Caroline, Peter, Heather, or Tim) and create a drawing that shows the character doing what he or she does best. Encourage young artists to include other aspects of the poem in their scenes as well. These drawings might be placed in strategic points above and around the readers when the poem is performed.

# Winter's Assistants

*By Jacqueline Sweeney*

Hush-a-hush-a Hush-a-hush!

Trees! Pay attention!
Get ready to bend.
Our winter fandango's
about to begin.

Here's Crystalline Caroline,
Lady in Lace:
such elegant twirling,
there's no need to race.

Here's Peter the Frost Painter,
Roof-Tapping Tim,
Road-Freezing Heather:
warm weather can't win!

Slog-slushing ice-crunching
now it begins:

roof-sagging limb-dragging
sled-slides-and-spins.

Snow-blowing co-co-ing
Time to come in?

Twig-snapping snow-swirling
whooshing of wind.

But Tim is roof-zapping
his sleet is tap-tapping,
while Caroline's snowflakes
are whirling through space.

Peter is frosting our windows all night
while Heather makes driving a fright.

There's ice in our nose hairs.
We can't feel our chins!
Foot-freezing   chest-wheezing
We should go in!

Such hush-a-hush whiteness
of beauty and brightness!

No, No, No
Stay-oh-stay
We can't go in!

We are cold snow-rollers
and packers and patters.
Rolling and rolling and
packing and patting

round snowballs, fat bellies
heads with no ears.
Our first snow creatures
begin to appear!

Add long twiggy fingers,
and tall pinecone ears,
and cookie mouths shouting out:

"Winter is here! Winter is here!"
Winter's Assistants say:

"Winter is here!"

# Winter's Assistants

*By Jacqueline Sweeney*

---

**PLAYERS:**     GROUP ONE: Readers 1–8

CHORUS: (Rest of the class)

---

**Reader 1:**     "Winter's Assistants"
by Jacqueline Sweeney

**CHORUS:**     *Hush-a-hush-a Hush-a-hush!*

**Reader 1:**     Trees! Pay attention!
Get ready to bend.

**Reader 2:**     Our winter fandango's
about to begin.

**Reader 3:**     Here's Crystalline Caroline,
Lady in Lace:

**Reader 4:**     such elegant twirling,
there's no need to race.

**Reader 1:**     Here's Peter the Frost Painter,

**Reader 2:**     Roof-Tapping Tim,

**Reader 3:**     Road-Freezing Heather:

**Reader 4:**     warm weather can't win!

**MORE** ➡

**Reader 5:** Slog-slushing ice-crunching
now it begins:

**Reader 6:** roof-sagging limb-dragging
sled-slides-and-spins.

**Reader 7:** Snow-blowing co-co-ing
Time to come in?

**Reader 8:** Twig-snapping snow-swirling
whooshing of wind.

**Reader 1:** But Tim is roof-zapping

**Reader 2:** his sleet is tap-tapping,

**Reader 3:** while Caroline's snowflakes

**Reader 4:** are whirling through space.

**Reader 1:** Peter is frosting our windows all night
while Heather makes driving a fright.

**Reader 5:** There's ice in our nose hairs.

**Reader 6:** We can't feel our chins!

**Reader 7:** Foot-freezing   chest-wheezing

**Reader 8:** We should go in!

**CHORUS:** *Such hush-a-hush whiteness*
of beauty and brightness!

**CHORUS:** *No, No, No*
*Stay-oh-stay,*
*We can't go in!*

**Reader 3:** We are cold snow-rollers

**Reader 4:** and packers and patters.

**Reader 3:** Rolling and rolling

**Reader 4:** and packing and patting

**Reader 5:** round snowballs, fat bellies
heads with no ears.

**Reader 6:** Our first snow creatures
begin to appear!

**Reader 7:** Add long twiggy fingers,
and tall pinecone ears,

**Reader 8:** and cookie mouths shouting out:

**All Readers:** "Winter is here!  Winter is here!"
Winter's Assistants say:

"Winter is here!"

**CHORUS:** *"Winter is here! Winter is here!*
*Wonderful winter*
*is finally here!"*

3

# Reading Tips

Talk to your students about how to read iambic tetrameter. Look at the rhythm of the first line together and read it aloud. "Four mountain peaks surround our town" (Ba-ba' Ba-ba' Ba-ba' Ba-ba').

The four readers are telling a story with this poem. Each of their voices is important in this poetic comparison between a grandmother's face and a mountain.

Consider asking students to add sound and movement as they read. For example, Reader 3 might pretend she's dabbing cold cream on her cheeks and chin. What other sounds and gestures could readers add?

For the final stanzas, Readers 3 and 4 should read their lines with emphasis and even exaggeration, for they are asking sincere, yet hilarious questions, which represent the comic turnaround in meaning for the poem.

# How to Teach "Mountain Face"

"Mountain Face" is an orderly poem written in iambic tetrameter. There are nine stanzas. Each stanza contains two lines of poetry, with four stressed syllables (beats) each. (In this poem, the second set of four beats is laid out in two parts, giving each stanza three lines.) All your students need to know is that the beats fall on the even syllables, like the gallop of an even-gaited horse.

## Questions to ask students:

**1.** The two main images compared in the poem are a grandmother's face and the surface of a mountain. Ask students if they can find word clues in the poem that describe either one or both. Write two headings on the board on a piece of chart paper: "Gram's Face" and "Mountain Face." Brainstorm this list together, adding words like *face*, *cracks*, *wrinkles*, *lines*, etc.

**2.** Explore the poem's use of adjectives, explaining how adjectives make a noun's meaning come alive, much as frosting and sprinkles make a plain cupcake become something precise and enticing. Consider the difference between a cupcake and a "gooey chocolate cupcake" or a "rainbow-sprinkled strawberry cupcake."

**3.** Ask students to refer to the text to find adjectives they can put in front of Gram's and the Mountain's face (i.e., *tree-lined*, *granite*).

**4.** Ask students who is speaking in the poem. How old do they think this speaker might be? Inquire about the poem's *tone* (the mood the poet wishes the audience to feel). Is it serious? Fun? What evidence can students find for their point of view?

## Extension Activity:

Ask students to download images from the Web or draw their own pictures of mountains—and then, carefully, turn them into faces, using their own artistic skills. You might expand this idea to other aspects of nature, such as the sky, rainbows, clouds, trees, bodies of water, etc. Invite students to use natural features whenever possible when creating their faces.

© 2014 Scholastic Inc. • Perfect Poetry Playlists • page 32

# Mountain Face

*By Jacqueline Sweeney*

Four mountain peaks surround our town.
Gram says they'll stand
when she's worn down.

She says each mountain has a face
with granite lines
we can't erase.

When Gram gets cold cream from a jar
and dabs it on
her cheeks and chin,

her face looks like a whipped cream pie
'til she smooths
 all her wrinkles in.

When winter snowstorms start to rage,
our mountains look like
Grandma's face,

and occupy such sky-filled space,
it has to snow for
nights and days

to cold-cream all the tree-lined cracks
and granite wrinkles
every place.

Do winter athletes realize
they're sledding down
a whipped cream pie?

Would skiers go some other place
if they knew they skied a
cold creamed face?

# Mountain Face

*By Jacqueline Sweeney*

**PLAYERS:**   Readers 1–4

**Reader 1:**   "Mountain Face"
by Jacqueline Sweeney

**Reader 1:**   Four mountain peaks surround our town.

**Reader 2:**   Gram says they'll stand
when she's worn down.

**Reader 1:**   She says each mountain has a face

**1**   **MORE** ➡

**Reader 2:**     with granite lines
we can't erase.

**Reader 3:**     When Gram gets cold cream from a jar
and dabs it on her cheeks and chin,

**Reader 4:**     Her face looks like a whipped cream pie
'til she smoothes all her wrinkles in.

**Reader 1:**     When winter snowstorms start to rage
our mountains look like Grandma's face,
and occupy such sky-filled space,

**Reader 2:**     it has to snow
for nights and days
to cold-cream all the tree-lined cracks
and granite wrinkles every place.

**Reader 3:**     Do winter athletes realize
they're sledding down
a whipped cream pie?

**Reader 4:**     Would skiers go some other place
if they knew they skied
a cold creamed face?

# Reading Tips

Many readers are needed for this poem. Two readers portray George Washington and Abraham Lincoln. More are needed for the chorus and the drums. If drums are not available, students can use clapping for rhythm.

This poem should be read with seriousness and dignity. Before your staged reading, have students research the terms and places mentioned in the poem so they can read with meaning. You may even want to have a group of students be your "class historians" who can share knowledge with the class on each reference.

# How to Teach "The Washington–Lincoln Chat"

"The Washington–Lincoln Chat" is an imagined conversation between our first and 16th presidents. With the poem, students can begin to think about how one president inspired another. Washington wanted to free the colonists from subservience to England and maintained that a house (or country) that is united cannot fall. Abraham Lincoln embraced this philosophical legacy by fighting to keep the country united during the Civil War. Both presidents seemed to be fighting against all odds and neither could be sure their cause would succeed.

## Questions to ask students:

**1.** This is a perfect poem to read on Presidents' Day. Talk about the two presidents. Ask students to share what they know. You might point out how each president was embroiled in war. How were these wars different? There are different issues of freedom for the two presidents. These will be important concepts as you study the poem.

**2.** Make a chart titled "George Washington and Abraham Lincoln" with headings labelled "Similarities" and "Differences." Invite students to search the poem for words and phrases to list in the respective columns. Which column is longer? Ask students to identify which qualities on the "Similarities" list helped make these two presidents so exceptional.

**3.** Ask students to search for the two direct quotes from George Washington and Abraham Lincoln within the body of the poem. Why is it important to hear their own words as well as those of the poet?

**4.** Talk with students about the way that poems often prompt us as readers to think and to feel. Ask them which parts of the poem bring out the most feeling.

**5.** Sometimes we forget that famous people were once children, too, with many of the same problems and issues faced by children of today. Can students make connections with any of the experiences of George Washington or Abraham Lincoln, such as shyness, personal struggles, or losing a loved one?

© 2014 Scholastic Inc. • Perfect Poetry Playlets • page 36

# The Washington–Lincoln Chat

*By Jacqueline Sweeney*

"It is better to offer no excuse than a bad one." —*George Washington*

"I have just tried to do my best each and every day." —*Abraham Lincoln*

"A real friend walks in when the rest of the world walks out." —*George Washington*

"To ease another's heartache is to forget one's own." —*Abraham Lincoln*

Long time away from home
Saratoga—Valley Forge
muskets—cannons—frozen toes
                    wages low

Many ladies lost their husbands.
Many parents lost their sons.

Long time away from home
Gettysburg—Bull Run
brothers fought brothers
fathers fought sons

Many ladies lost their husbands.
Many parents lost their sons.

| | |
|---|---|
| Abe: | For Freedom! |
| George: | For Liberty! |
| George: | How to MAKE our country free |
| Abe: | How to KEEP our country free |
| George: | From England! |
| Abe: | From Slavery! |
| George: | Revolution! |
| Abe: | North and South! |
| George & Abe: | We wanted Peace and Unity. |
| George: | A house UNITED cannot fall. |
| Abe: | I did NOT want our house to fall. |
| G & A: | Look at us! |
| George: | Silver hair and spectacles. |
| Abe: | Constant worries—lack of sleep |
| George: | Ill health—wooden teeth? HIPPO teeth! |
| Abe: | War will do this to a man |
| George: | And being President! |
| Abe: | I felt I knew you. |
| George: | I wish I'd known you. I'd have told you many things. |

# The Washington–Lincoln Chat (Continued)

Abe: You did! I read your book by candlelight.

You inspired me.

George: I'm flattered, sir.

We are alike in many ways.

Abe: I hear you never told a lie.

George: Not true!

But the most enviable of all titles is the character of an honest man.

George: I hear they called you 'Honest Abe.'

Abe: When I do good I feel good.

When I do bad I feel bad.

G & A: We are alike in many ways.

Abe: Mom died when I was nine.

George: Dad died when I was ten.

G & A: Sad times . . . sad times.

Abe: Rail splitter!

George: Surveyor!

Abe: Book Reader!

George: Farmer!

Abe: Lawyer!

George: Soldier!

Abe: At first I was shy.

George: So was I!!!

Abe: Didn't want the role of leader.

George: Didn't want to be the FIRST.

G & A: But we wanted UNITY. And Peace.

George: Too bad peace required war.

Abe: War split our country..... and our hearts.

George: War always splits the heart.

Abe: I hear you took no pay until the war was won. Nobly done, sir Nobly done.

George: I fought on many battle-fields facing many guns.

You faced only one— a mad man's gun, and died as war was won. You, sir, are the noble one.

Abe: I wish you'd been my father.

George: I wish you'd been my son.

# The Washington– Lincoln Chat

*By Jacqueline Sweeney*

| **PLAYERS:** | Readers: 1–14 |
| --- | --- |
| | George Washington's Chorus (Readers 1–7) |
| | Abraham Lincoln's Chorus (Readers 8–14) |
| | Drummers (4–6 students) |

**Directions:**
Two chairs stage front for George and Abe.
Each has their chorus standing behind them.
Drummers sit in between the two choruses.

**Reader 1:**    "The Washington–Lincoln Chat"
by Jacqueline Sweeney

*(Drummers begin stately drumbeat.
Ba-Ba-ba'ba'ba'-Ba
Repeat three times loudly and then continue
very softly as readers speak.)*

**Reader 1:**    "It is better to offer no excuse
than a bad one."

**Reader 8:**    "I have just tried to do my best
each and every day."

I          **MORE**  ▶

**Reader 2:** "A real friend walks in when the rest of the world walks out."

**Reader 9:** "To ease another's heartache is to forget one's own." *(Drumbeats get louder for a moment, then softer again.)*

**Reader 3:** Long time away from home

**Reader 4:** Saratoga!

**Reader 5:** Valley Forge!

**Reader 6:** muskets—cannons—frozen toes

**Reader 7:** wages low

**Both Choruses:** Many ladies lost their husbands.
Many parents lost their sons.

**Reader 10:** Long time away from home

**Reader 11:** Gettysburg!

**Reader 12:** Bull Run!

**Reader 13:** brothers fought brothers

**Reader 14:** fathers fought sons

**Both Choruses:** Many ladies lost their husbands.
Many parents lost their sons.

© 2014 Scholastic Inc. • Perfect Poetry Playlets • page 40

**Abe Enters:**        FOR FREEDOM!

**George Enters:**      FOR LIBERTY!

**George:**             How to MAKE our country free

**Abe:**               How to KEEP our country free

**George:**             From England!

**Abe:**               From Slavery!

**George:**             Revolution!

**Abe:**               North and South!

**George's Chorus:**   Freedom from England! Revolution!

**Abe's Chorus:**      Freedom from Slavery! North and South!

*(Drummers stop drumming as Abe sits down.)*

**George & Abe:**     We wanted Peace and Unity.

**George:**             A house UNITED cannot fall.

**George's Chorus:**   A house UNITED cannot fall.

**Abe:**               I did NOT want our house to fall.

**Abe's Chorus:**      Did NOT want our house to fall.

**George & Abe:**     Look at us!

**George:**             Silver hair and spectacles.

| | |
|---|---|
| **Abe:** | Constant worries—lack of sleep. |
| **Abe's Choruses:** | No sleep! No sleep! |
| **George:** | Ill health—wooden teeth? HIPPO teeth! |
| **George's Choruses:** | Spectacles and Hippo teeth! |
| **Abe:** | War will do this to a man. |
| **George:** | And being President!<br>*(Both men pause.)* |
| **Abe:** | I felt I knew you. |
| **George:** | I wish I'd known you.<br>I'd have told you many things. |
| **Abe:** | You did! I read your book by candlelight.<br>You inspired me. |
| **George:** | I'm flattered, sir.<br>We are alike in many ways. |
| **Both Choruses:** | many ways... many ways... |
| **Abe:** | I hear you never told a lie. |
| **George:** | Not true!<br>But the most enviable of all titles<br>is the character of an honest man.<br>I hear they called you 'Honest Abe.' |

**Abe:** When I do good I feel good.
When I do bad I feel bad.

**George & Abe:** We are alike in many ways.

**Both Choruses:** many ways.....many ways...

**Abe:** Mom died when I was nine.

**George:** Dad died when I was ten.

**Both Choruses:** Sad times... sad times...

**Abe:** Rail splitter!
*(Abe points at himself.)*

**George:** Surveyor!
*(George points at himself.)*

**Abe:** Book Reader!

**George:** Farmer!

**Abe:** Lawyer!

**George:** Soldier!

**Abe:** At first I was shy.

**George:** So was I.

**Abe:** Didn't want the role of leader.

**George:** Didn't want to be the FIRST.

| **Both Choruses:** | Not the leader. Not the FIRST... |
|---|---|
| **Abe & George:** | But we wanted UNITY. And Peace. |
| **George:** | Too bad peace required war. |
| **Abe:** | War split our country... and our hearts. |
| **George:** | War always splits the heart. |
| **Both Choruses:** | Always the heart |

**Abe:**
I hear you took no pay
until the war was won.
Nobly done, sir.
Nobly done.

**George:**
I fought on many battlefields facing many guns.
You faced only one—a mad man's gun,
and died as war was won.
You, sir, are the noble one.

*(Both men pause.)*

**Abe:** I wish you'd been my father.

**George:** I wish you'd been my son.

*(Both men bow their heads.)*

*(Drummers begin drumming slowly again until everyone leaves the stage, then abruptly stop, stand up, and walk out silently together).*

## Reading Tips

This poem is set up for six readers, but can easily be modified at your discretion to have any number of readers from one to 14, depending on how the lines and stanzas are divided.

Encourage readers to speak clearly and loudly. The pacing should speed up with the third stanza. Readers can offer a hint of excitement with animal and leaf rustling sounds. By the time the fifth stanza arrives, the words should be almost whispered, as if the child on the other side of the window might be awakened too soon. (Loud, stage whispers, of course!) Readers 1 and 2 should pop up from their crouching positions one at a time as they read their parts.

The final stanza should be handled with delicacy. A child is waking up. Reader 5 stands up slowly, yawning, rubbing sleep from his eyes, remaining standing after speaking his lines. Reader 6 should leap up from her crouch with arms wide while loudly exclaiming "sunrise!" This is the pivotal event in the poem. Reader 5 then slowly and seriously informs the audience that the Moon is gone.

# How to Teach "Moon Poem"

"Moon Poem" is an image poem. In it, the moon's light shines on things to tell a small story. It is like a photographic journey with the moon as a lighted camera.

## Questions to ask students:

**1.** Have students look at the first and last stanza of the poem. What is happening in stanza one? What is happening in stanza seven? Ask if they can see how the middle stanzas move the poem forward until it is time to end the poem.

**2.** This poem could be considered a list poem. The poet has carefully selected specific nouns for the moon to shine upon. Ask students to focus on the middle stanzas. Could the poet have made different noun choices and still have created the same effect in the end? This is a good time to talk about how poets create a world for the reader to inhabit for a brief moment and how their choices are important.

**3.** Call your students attention to stanza three. What is different about this stanza? How does the shift to verbs and sounds change the tempo of these lines?

**4.** Ask your students to locate the rhymes in this poem. The pattern is consistent, every second and fourth line. Explain that rhyme was used before printing presses, to help people remember the words to poems, and often these poems were either accompanied by a musical instrument, such as the lute or harp, or performed as a song.

## Extension Activity:

Try having students create their own list poems. Begin by writing a class poem in which the word *Sun* is repeated in the same pattern as *Moon* in "Moon Poem." Begin and end with the sun rising and setting. Together, decide what you wish your sunlight to shine upon, carefully choosing each word with a picture in mind for the readers' minds to see and enjoy as they hear the poem. Then, have students work on their own list poems about whatever they like—anything from "Things That Fit in a Pocket to Places I Want to Visit Someday."

# Moon Poem

*By Jacqueline Sweeney*

Moon rise
Moon light
Moon gleam
Moon bright

Moon trees
Moon pond
Moon silver
Moon swan

Moon hoot
Moon howl
Moon rustle
Moon growl

Moon turtle
Moon breeze
Moon slither
Moon leaves

Moon house
Moon lawn
Moon freckles
Moon fawn

Moon window
Moon beam
Moon child
Moon dream

Moon eyes
Moon yawn
Sun RISE
Moon
     g
      o
       n
        e

# Moon Poem

*By Jacqueline Sweeney*

**PLAYERS:**   Readers 1–6

**Reader 1:**    "Moon Poem"
by Jacqueline Sweeney

**Reader 1:**    Moon rise
Moon light
Moon gleam
Moon bright

**Reader 2:**    Moon trees
Moon pond
Moon silver
Moon swan

**Reader 3:**    Moon hoot
Moon howl

**Reader 4:**    Moon rustle
Moon growl

**Reader 5:**    Moon turtle
Moon breeze

**Reader 6:**    Moon slither
Moon leaves

**1**          **MORE** ➤

**Reader 1:**     Moon house
                  Moon lawn

**Reader 2:**     Moon freckles
                  Moon fawn

**Reader 3:**     Moon window
                  Moon beam

**Reader 4:**     Moon child
                  Moon dream

**Reader 5:**     Moon eyes
                  Moon yawwwwn

**Reader 6:**     Sun RISE

**Reader 5:**     Moon
                    g
                     o
                       n
                        e

2

## Reading Tips

The readers should begin as a rainstorm begins—slowly at first. The rhymed stanzas 2, 3, and 4 are telling the rain's story. The pace should accelerate as the readers pop out their lines. Keep the momentum going from one reader to the next. Zappity zip—one line should rapidly follow another.

Ask readers to keep tongue twisters in mind as they read out the alliterated sounds in the fifth stanza.

The rest of the poem should be a joyful declaration of personal power. The phrase "squooshes to MUD" can be repeated in chorus by all ten readers as often as needed— as one by one, the readers "oozily" lower themselves to the floor.

# How to Teach "Listen!"

Right from the start, it is apparent that "Listen!" is meant to be fun. Its zippy sound effects (onomatopoeia) border on slapstick in the final stanzas, allowing young readers to revel in silliness.

## Questions to ask students:

**1.** Ask your young readers: *What do you think is the significance of the title? How does it set up the commanding tone of the poem?*

**2.** Ask students who is speaking in the poem. Can they see how the rain starts out with the power, and the speaker of the poem ends up with it?

**3.** Have students identify the rhyme pattern. How does it move the poem along?

**4.** Ask students the meaning of the word *trauma* in the third stanza. Why is rain a trauma for cats? Are there other ways rain might be a trauma for other animals? Perhaps some students can share how rain has sometimes been a trauma for them.

**5.** Talk about the *onomatopoeia* in the poem. Have students list all the sound words they can find in the poem. Call their attention to the alliteration (repeated initial consonant sounds). Perhaps students can circle the repeated letter sounds to show how onomatopoeia and alliteration sometimes work together.

## Extension Activity:

Invite students to write their own sound poems filled with "noisy words." Begin by brainstorming a list of noisy places: a school lunchroom, inside a popcorn popper, the mall at Christmas, an ambulance ride. Have students work on poems that convey the sounds of the place they chose as their subject.

# LISTEN!

*By Jacqueline Sweeney*

The rain hits the puddles *pop-pop-plop!*
pings the roof *spat-a-tat-tat!*
baps the leaves *pip-plip-drip!*
slaps the ground *woppity-thud!*

The rain
washes windows,
makes playgrounds for frogs,
sings babies to sleep,
brings bath time to hogs.

The rain kisses roses,
umbrellas, and hats.
It makes life a trauma
for sun-loving cats.

The rain has the power
to be quite a pain
when cancelling recess
and all outdoor games.

So with all of its sopping
and spitting and slopping,
and splat-a-tat-tatting
and woppity-thuds,

the rain makes me happy
when splatting is snappy,

And I can splash puddles
that splish, splosh and flood.

'Cause I am the master
of puddle *DISASTER*

*that smoozily-oozily*
*squooshes to*

  *MUD!*

# LISTEN!

*By Jacqueline Sweeney*

**PLAYERS:**   Readers 1–10

**Reader 4:**   "Listen!"
by Jacqueline Sweeney

**Reader 1:**   The rain hits the puddles

**Reader 2:**   pop-pop-plop!

**Reader 3:**   pings the roof

**Reader 4:**   spat-a-tat-tat!

**Reader 1:**   baps the leaves

**Reader 2:**   pip-plip-drip!

**Reader 3:**   slaps the ground

**Reader 4:**   woppity-thud!

**Reader 5:**   The rain washes windows,

**Reader 6:**   makes playgrounds for frogs,

**Reader 7:**   sings babies to sleep,

**MORE**

**Reader 8:**   brings bath time to hogs.

**Reader 5:**   The rain kisses roses,
umbrellas, and hats.

**Reader 6:**   It makes life a trauma
for sun-loving cats.

**Reader 7:**   The rain has the power
to be quite a pain

**Reader 8:**   when cancelling recess
and all outdoor games.

**Reader 9:**   So with all of its sopping
and spitting and slopping,

**Reader 10:**   and splat-a-tat-tatting
and woppity-thuds,

**Reader 9:**   the rain makes me happy
when splatting is snappy,

**Reader 10:**   And I can splash puddles
that splish, splosh and flood.

**Reader 9:**   'Cause I am the master
of puddle DISASTER

**Reader 10:**   that smoozily-oozily
squooshes to
MUD!

**All Readers:**   squooshes to MUD
squooshes to MUD
smoozily-oozily
squooshes to MUD!

## Reading Tips

Readers should keep in mind that the movement in this poem is carried by its verbs, and these should be accented on the second syllable and affirmed:
ba–bá
"I'd kneel"
"and flap."

The pace will speed up with "gulping one last gulp . . ." until "loop and climb." On the last lines, the voice should rise and fall just like the kite.

All the readers should pounce on the word *soar*, which is the most important verb in the poem and signifies the final action of freedom for the kite as it breaks free to enter "pure sky."

Each reader might repeat the words "pure sky" as he or she pretends to sail out of the reading space.

# How to Teach "Being a Kite"

"Being a Kite" is a poem about dreaming of soaring and flying like a kite. The kite is personified with human qualities in a sustained comparison known as an *extended metaphor*. An extended metaphor is also known as a *conceit*, a metaphor dynamo that contains many smaller comparisons within itself.

## Questions to ask students:

**1.** Begin by talking about *similes* and *metaphors*. Share a few similes (comparisons using *like* or *as*) with your class, such as "My hair is like spaghetti." Then, remove the *like* or *as* from each comparison and ask your students, *Does the meaning change?* Help them see that a metaphor is often a stronger assertion.

**2.** Ask students to find the comparisons between person and kite. Consider having students draw a box around each new stanza using a different color for each box, so they can easily see the changing comparisons.

**3.** Have students think about the structure of the poem—the way it looks on the page. How do the words in the final stanzas look different from the other stanzas? How does this change in structure reinforce meaning?

## Extension Activity:

Allow students to write their own "If I were" poems, choosing whatever object they'd like to be, and hence, personify. The children might imagine they really are the object, and then make a list of verbs that answer the question: "If I were a _____, what would I do?"

# Being a Kite

*By Jacqueline Sweeney*

If I were a kite
I'd kneel,
stretch my skinny arms
out wide,
and wait for wind.

My yellow shirt would
fill up like a sail
and flap,
tugging my criss-crossed
wooden bones and me
towards seas of cloud.

My rippling paper skin
would rustle like applause
as I inhaled,
gulping one last gust
to swoop me giddy-quick
above the trees.

My red rag tail
would drift
toward everything green
to balance me

so all day
I could
loop and climb
loop
and climb
and *SOAR*
into pure sky.

# Being a Kite

*By Jacqueline Sweeney*

**PLAYERS:**     Readers 1–4

**Reader 1:**     "Being a Kite"
by Jacqueline Sweeney

**Reader 1:**     If I were a kite
I'd kneel,
stretch my skinny arms out wide,
and wait for wind.

**Reader 2:**     My yellow shirt
would fill up like a sail
and flap,
tugging my criss-crossed wooden bones
and me
towards seas of cloud.

**Reader 3:**     My rippling paper skin
would rustle like applause
as I inhaled,

I               **MORE** ➤

**Reader 4:** gulping one last gust
to swoop me giddy-quick
above the trees.

**Reader 3:** My red rag tail
would drift
toward everything green
to balance me

**Reader 4:** So all day
I could
loop and climb
loop
and climb

**All Readers:** and *SOAR*
into pure sky.

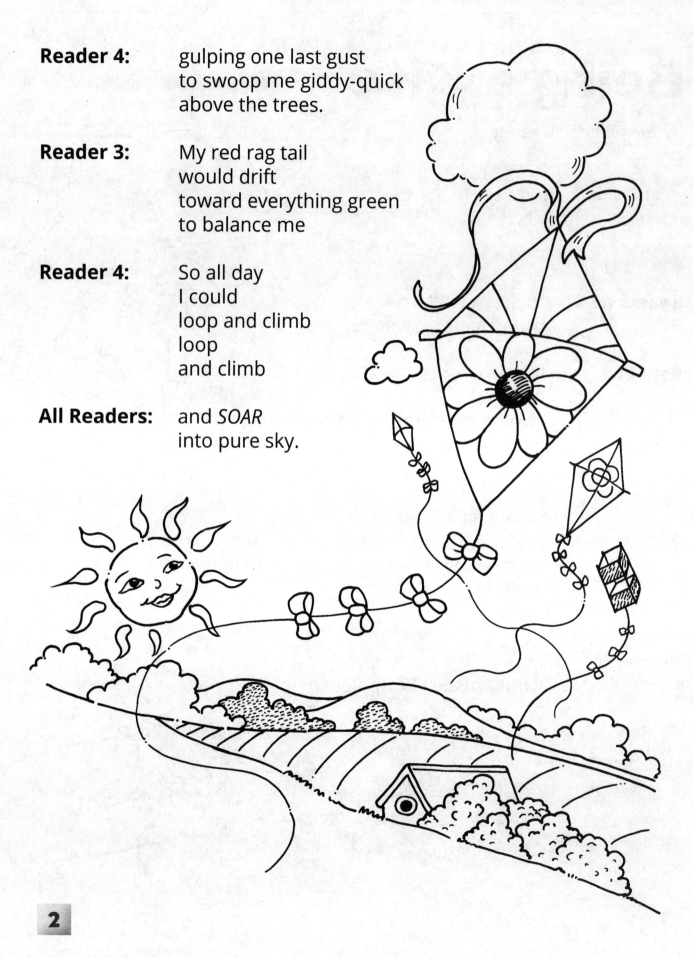

## Reading Tips

This poem is voiced for six readers. The beginning lines should be read at a slow, rhythmic pace that begins to pick up speed with the question: "What's this?"

The fifth stanza is filled with a fast flurry of adjectives "fast-flying, line-driving, feathers and all." Explain to students that the hyphens between these words indicate that they should be read swiftly, with the entire phrase screeching towards the audience like a fast-pitched baseball.

The final line—"How could he think that a bird was a ball!"—should be exclaimed loudly by both readers, and then the audience might join in repeating it softly until all the readers exit the staging area—shaking their heads in dismay as they slink away.

# How to Teach "First Time at Third"

"First Time at Third" is about baseball, of course. A player is so eager to catch a flyball that he accidentally tries to catch something else entirely to his great embarrassment.

## Questions to ask students:

**1.** Ask students: *Have you ever seen or experienced an embarrassing moment during a sport or activity? What happened? How did you feel? What happened next? What would you do differently if you could change any part of this experience?*

**2.** Explain that a poet's job is to make us feel a part of the poetic experience. Reading a poem gives us the opportunity to share in an experience or deep feelings. Sometimes, it's a moment bigger than ourselves, a moment in history, perhaps, and sometimes it's a simple everyday happening.

**3.** Point out the author's use of strong verbs. Have students make a list of all the verbs in the poem, and then circle the ones they think have the most power.

**4.** Call students' attention to the questions in the poem, such as "Will it ever begin?" and "The game hasn't started?" What feelings do these questions convey? Frustration? Impatience? You might also ask: *To whom are these questions addressed?*

## Extension Activity:

Ask students to think of an embarrassing moment they feel comfortable enough to share. Suggest they choose an event from their past that seems funny to them now, but was not funny then. Next, have them write about this moment in prose or poetry format. Ask students to describe what happened in a step-by-step manner that includes details: before the event, during the event, and after the event. Later, students who wish to share their stories, can read them aloud and laugh at past errors.

# First Time at Third

*By Jacqueline Sweeney*

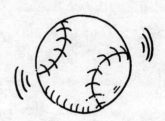

First time at third
nothing but nerves.
He fist-whomps his glove,
tucks in his shirt,
kicks up the dirt
for the twenty-fifth time.

Gets in position
pumped up to win,
ump sweeps the plate.
Will it ever begin?

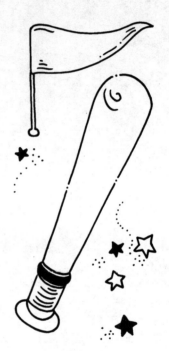

A quick line-drive!
He leaps for the sky.
His body's an arrow,
glove aimed high.

What's this?
He stumbles,
he tumbles to earth.
His glove is still empty,
face red as his shirt.

The game hasn't started?
"Play ball!" can be heard
and he's tried to snag
a low flying bird;
fast-flying, line-driving
feathers and all.

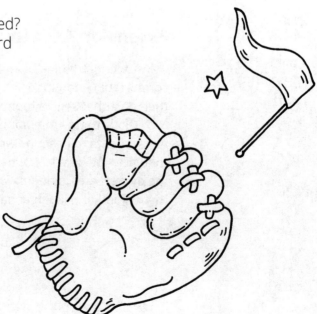

How could he think
that a bird was a ball!

# First Time at Third

*By Jacqueline Sweeney*

**PLAYERS:**   Readers 1–6

**Reader 1:**   "First Time at Third"
by Jacqueline Sweeney

**Reader 1:**   First time at third
nothing but nerves.

**Reader 2:**   He fist-whomps his glove,
tucks in his shirt,
kicks up the dirt
for the twenty-fifth time.

**Reader 1:**   Gets in position
pumped up to win,

**Reader 2:**   ump sweeps the plate.
Will it ever begin?

**Reader 3:**   A quick line-drive!
He leaps for the sky.

**1**        **MORE** ➡

**Reader 4:** His body's an arrow,
glove aimed high.

**Reader 3:** What's this?
He stumbles,
he tumbles to earth.

**Reader 4:** His glove is still empty,
face red as his shirt.

**Reader 5:** The game hasn't started?

**Reader 6:** "Play ball!" can be heard

**Reader 5:** and he's tried to snag
a low-flying bird;

**Reader 6:** fast-flying, line-driving
feathers and all.

**All Readers:** *fast-flying, line-driving*
*feathers and all.*

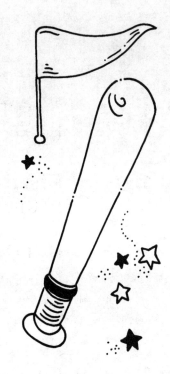

**Readers 5 & 6:** How could he think
that a bird was a ball!

**All Readers:** HOW COULD HE THINK
THAT A BIRD WAS A BALL!

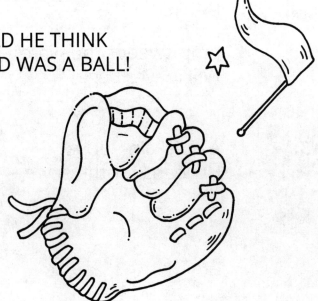

© 2014 Scholastic Inc. • Perfect Poetry Playlets • page 60

## Reading Tips

Because "Choose a Color" is written in couplets, the voices in this reading can easily be rearranged at the your discretion to include up to 10 readers working in pairs.

It is a short poem. Explain to your readers that every line is important and should be read slowly and carefully so listeners can picture each image in their minds. Explain that the ending is most significant, as the entire poem moves towards this point.

The ending lines "If green I would help the world breathe" can be repeated several times, in a chorus.

# How to Teach "Choose a Color"

"Choose a Color" is a versatile poem that celebrates colors in nature. It is a wonderful poem to share for Earth Day.

## Questions to ask students:

**1.** This poem is mostly written in couplets. Ask students to find places in the poem where the couplet format changes, as in the quatrain (four lines) about silver. See if anyone notices the single lines "tree canopied" and "breathe." These lines are set apart because of their significance.

**2.** Introduce the use of conditional tense, specifically the use of *were* and *would* in these couplet formations. Try substituting the word *was* for *were* and ask if anyone can hear the difference in meaning

## Extension Activity:

Have students write their own versions of this poem. For each color, students can fill in their own choices of what they would be if they were orange or yellow or blue or green.

# Choose a Color

*By Jacqueline Sweeney*

If I were brown I'd be a cattail
or turtle deep burrowed
in mud.

If I were orange I'd be a
newt's belly,

If yellow a willow
in fall.

If pink I'd be a flamingo
or salmon leaping
upstream.

If I were blue I'd be
glacier,

If purple a larkspur
in spring.

If I were silver I'm
sure I'd be river
*moonshattered* in
liquid surprise.

If I were green I'd be
rainforest,

tree canopied.

If green I would help the
world

breathe.

# Choose a Color

*By Jacqueline Sweeney*

**PLAYERS:**    Readers 1–6

**Reader 1:**    "Choose a Color"
by Jacqueline Sweeney

**Reader 2:**    If I were brown I'd be a cattail

**Reader 3:**    or turtle deep burrowed in mud.

**Reader 4:**    If I were orange I'd be a newt's belly,

**Reader 5:**    If yellow a willow in fall.

**Reader 6:**    If pink I'd be a flamingo

**Reader 1:**    or salmon leaping upstream.

**Reader 2:**    If I were blue I'd be glacier,

**Reader 3:**    If purple a larkspur in spring.

**Reader 4:**    If I were silver I'm sure I'd be river
*moonshattered* in liquid surprise.

**Reader 5:**    If I were green I'd be rainforest,
*tree canopied*

**Reader 6:**    If GREEN, I would help the world BREATHE.

**All:**    If green, I would help the world breathe.

## Reading Tips

These little playlets are designed for participation by an entire class, so any extra students can be placed in a chorus role. The actors for polliwog, snake, and turtles will perform the action as the readers present the lines.

For the polliwog poem, chorus voices should begin low and steady, progressively becoming louder, until the chorus is shouting joyful repetitions of "There goes our frog!" at the end.

For the snake poem, the chorus should remain detached and steady throughout, with almost deadpan voices and faces.

For the turtles poem, the chorus echoes the tone of the readers. The readers set the tone in this piece, and the chorus will take their cues from them. The final onomatopoeia in each poem should be said loudly and joyfully by all the readers and chorus.

# How to Teach "Who's in the Bog?"

"Who's in the Bog?" is a three-part poem featuring creatures that are often found in this damp habitat—frogs, snakes, and turtles. All of the creatures of the bog are undergoing change: A polliwog is metamorphosing into a frog, a snake is shedding its skin, and turtle eggs are becoming hatchlings. This poem is specifically designed as a vehicle for older children to perform for the younger grades.

## Questions to ask students:

**1.** Review the term *metamorphosis* with students, as well as the life cycles and habits of snakes, turtles, and frogs. Better yet, ask students to do their own research and present it back to the class.

**2.** Ask students: *How is each poem different? How are they similar? Which parts rely more on onomatopoeia to characterize their animals?*

**3.** Talk about the importance of the *chorus* in literature. The role of the chorus dates back to ancient Greece. Then, as now, the role of the chorus was to comment on the action of the play or poem and help make clear to the audience the significance of event. Chorus members traditionally stood together alongside the action happening on stage and spoke in unison. Ask students how they think these poem playlets would sound without the chorus parts.

**4.** A Fun Fact: An ancient Greek poet named Aristophanes wrote a play called "The Frogs" in which frogs played the key role of the chorus. Their onomatopoeia sounds were: brek—ke—ke—kek ko—ax ko—ax. Do you think the frogs in ancient Greece sounded different from the frogs of today?

## Extension Activity:

Design and make costumes for your class performance. Keep it simple: large green shirts and paper masks for frogs, for example. Paint turtle shells on large pieces of brown paper. Then, perform the poem play for younger grades.

# Who's in the Bog?

*By Jacqueline Sweeney*

Polliwog wiggles
her body and tail
not yet a frog
　　　*not yet a frog*

She grows hind legs
and swims like a whale
still not a frog
　　　*still not a frog*

She sings her first song
and hops down the trail
Really a frog!
　　　*Really a frog!*

galunk-galunk-galunk-galunk
there goes our frog...
　　　*there goes our frog...*

Snake flicks his tongue
as he lays in the sun
in and out
　　　out and in

He squeezes through holes,
and rocks, and logs
in and out
　　　*out and in*

stretching and shedding
old, papery skin
that lays like a wrapper
that snake was in
　　　*from shade to sunlight*
　　　*out and in*
　　　*S-S-S out*
　　　*S-S-S in*

He slides to the bog
in his tight, new skin
happy to be in his
bright, new skin
　　　*in his tight new*
　　　*bright new skin*
　　　*HISSSS!*

Turtle eggs rest in
a hole in the ground
waiting to hatch
　　　*waiting to hatch*

Covered with leaves
so they cannot be found
safe 'til they hatch
　　　*safe 'til they hatch*

Push! Push!
Wiggle and push
push! push!
　　　*wiggle and push!*

Flip! Flop!
The babies flip-flop
flippity-floppity
　　　*flop-flop-flop!*

Small flippers unfold,
Necks stretch in surprise.
Egg shells behind them,
they've opened their eyes!

Scoot! Scoot!
They're on their way home,
scoot! scoot!
　　　*scoot! scoot!*

hurrying home
to the safe, wet bog

scurrying home
to the bog.

　　*Plip! Plip!*
　　　*plip-plip-plip*

　　*plippity!*
　　　*plippity!*
　　　*plip!*

# Who's in the Bog?

*By Jacqueline Sweeney*

> **PLAYERS:** Readers 1–8
> Chorus

**Reader 1:** "Who's in the Bog?" by Jacqueline Sweeney

**Reader 2:** Polliwog wiggles her body and tail

**Chorus:** *Not yet a frog*
*NOT YET A FROG*

**Reader 3:** She grows hind legs and swims like a whale

**Chorus:** *Still not a frog*
*STILL NOT A FROG*

**Reader 4:** She sings her first song and hops down the trail

**MORE**

| | |
|---|---|
| **Chorus:** | *REALLY A FROG!*<br>*REALLY A FROG!* |
| **Reader 5:** | galunk—galunk—galunk—galunk |
| **Both readers plus Chorus:** | *THERE GOES OUR FROG...*<br>*THERE GOES OUR FROG...*<br>*(Repeat until frog is out of sight.)* |
| **Reader 6:** | Snake flicks his tongue as he lays in the sun |
| **Chorus:** | *In and out*<br>*OUT AND IN* |
| **Reader 7:** | He squeezes through holes, and rocks, and logs |
| **Chorus:** | *In and out*<br>*OUT AND IN* |
| **Reader 8:** | stretching and shedding old, papery skin<br>that lays like a wrapper that snake was in |
| **Chorus:** | *FROM SHADE TO SUNLIGHT*<br>*OUT AND IN*<br>*S-S-S OUT*<br>*S-S-S IN* |
| **Reader 1:** | He slides to the bog in his tight, new skin,<br>happy to be in his bright, new skin |
| **Chorus:** | *IN HIS TIGHT NEW*<br>*BRIGHT NEW SKIN*<br>*(Repeat until snake slithers away.)* |
| **All:** | **HISSSSS!** |

**Reader 2:**   Turtle eggs rest in a hole in the ground

**Chorus:**   *Waiting to hatch*
*WAITING TO HATCH*

**Reader 3:**   Covered with leaves so they cannot be found

**Chorus:**   *Safe 'til they hatch*
*SAFE 'TIL THEY HATCH*

**Reader 4:**   Push! Push! Wiggle and push

**Chorus:**   *PUSH! PUSH!*
*WIGGLE AND PUSH!*

**Reader 5:**   Flip! Flop! The babies flip-flop

**Chorus:**   *FLIPPITY-FLOPPITY*
*FLOP—FLOP—FLOP!*

**Reader 6:**   Small flippers unfold, necks stretch in surprise.
Egg shells behind them, they've opened their eyes!

**Reader 6:**   Scoot! Scoot! They're on their way home

**Chorus:**   *SCOOT! SCOOT! SCOOT! SCOOT!*

**Reader 7:**   hurrying home to the safe, wet bog

**Reader 8:**   scurrying home to the bog.

**Chorus:**   *PLIP! PLIP!*
*PLIP—PLIP—PLIP*

**All:**   *PLIPPITY! PLIPPITY! PLIP!*
*(Repeat until all turtles scurry away.)*

3

## Reading Tips

There is a dreamy tone to this poem and the words should roll slowly, like the movement of a Ferris wheel. The line that breaks the reverie of the speaker should be read with abruptness: "'You're five,' Dad said."

Stanza four should be read with sputtering excitement. This child can't and won't let the night's images go.

The line, "as Dad drove slowly home," should be read slowly—like a ride in a dull, slow moving car.

The last stanza should be read strongly with determination.

# How to Teach "Ferris Wheel"

"Ferris Wheel" is a gentle poem about a past memory. It's like a mini-memoir in rhyme with a beginning, middle, and end.

## Questions to ask students:

**1.** Ask the class: *Who is speaking in the poem? Are there word clues in the text to indicate if the speaker is a boy or girl? If not, does it matter?*

**2.** Invite students to share their own experiences with Ferris wheels. What did they see? Feel? Hear? Then, go back to the poem and ask students to search for word clues that show them what is occurring from the narrator's point of view, such as sentences beginning with: "I rode…," "I heard…," "I felt…."

**3.** Point out the poet's use of simple verbs to tell the story, verbs a child might use. You might also point out the shift in structure in the first stanza: "around past clouds…," etc. Ask students why they think the author spaced the words this way. Consider writing the same words in sentence form and comparing the two to illustrate the visual power of structure in a poem.

**4.** Look closely at stanza four. Why is the word *music* in italics? How is the word *orbit* generally used? How does this word convey the wonder of a first Ferris wheel ride? What are the "dazzling bits of colored light?"

**5.** Turn attention to final stanza. What words indicate there's been a shift in time? Do students notice the change in tense from past to future— from "I rode" to "I'll ride?" What does "Van Gogh galaxies" bring to mind? Show your students an image of Vincent Van Gogh's painting *Starry Night*.

## Extension Activity:

Ask your students to write a poem about a first experience. It could be riding a roller coaster or a two-wheeler, a first home run, a dance recital. Ask your writers to begin their lines with simple verbs: "I saw…," "I heard…," "I feel…,"

# Ferris Wheel

*By Jacqueline Sweeney*

I rode the giant Ferris wheel.
My father held my hand.
I felt I rode around the world
from sky to trees
to land;
      around
          past clouds
         around
            past trees
        past mom
      waving
    with a shout.

I rode until the stars came out.
I rode until the wheel ran out of
music, and all the moving
stopped.

I left the Ferris wheel that night.
I didn't want to go.
 "You're five." Dad said, "It's time for bed."

But I heard *music* in my head.
I felt the orbit and the height,
the dazzling bits
of colored light,
as Dad drove slowly
      home.

Someday I'll ride that wheel again.
I want to glide and rock
around the world past clouds and trees,
past Van Gogh galaxies
of dreams;
a never ending glide and rock
I'll *never* want to stop!

# Ferris Wheel

*by Jacqueline Sweeney*

**PLAYERS:**   READERS: 1– 4

**Reader 1:**   "Ferris Wheel" by Jacqueline Sweeney

**Reader 2:**   I rode the giant Ferris wheel.
My father held my hand.
I felt I rode around the world
from sky to trees to land;

**Reader 3:**   around past clouds
around past trees
past Mom waving with a shout.

**Reader 4:**   I rode until the stars came out.
I rode until the wheel ran out of music,
and all the moving stopped.

**Reader 1:** I left the Ferris wheel that night.
I didn't want to go.
"You're five," Dad said, "It's time for bed."

**Reader 2:** But I heard music in my head.
I felt the orbit and the height,
the dazzling bits of colored light,
as Dad drove slowly home.

**Reader 3:** Someday I'll ride that wheel again.
I want to glide and rock
around the world past clouds and trees,
past Van Gogh galaxies of dreams;

**Reader 4:** a never ending glide and rock

**All:** I'll *never* want to stop!

## Reading Tips

The job of the first three readers is to handle the assertions in the poem, so they should boldly state the words in an even rhythm. The last two readers show us the step-by-step sequence of what happens next, and each reader is a part of this sequence and mustn't rush the words. The initial readers reappear to read the fantasy wish with great enthusiasm, trumpeting the wish with a shout.

The poem's ending can be extended, with each reader shouting "I want to swim!" while peeling off from the group one by one—like synchronized swimmers—until all the readers are sitting quietly on the floor.

# How to Teach "I Want to Swim"

Why do people write poems? Where do poets get their ideas? These are questions you might put before your class prior to reading this poem. Poets write about things that matter to them—events in their lives, the world, marvels of nature. They write about things that make them feel so deeply that they want to shout their feelings out. And words can shout even about quiet things like roses, shyness, and stars.

## Questions to ask students:

**1.** Look closely at the word *really* in this poem. What is the difference between swimming and *really* swimming? Ask your children if they remember a time when they could not manage to succeed at something they really wanted to do—like whistle, or play a difficult game, or skateboard?

**2.** Point out the rhythm commanding the first two stanzas. The meter is like an encouraging drumbeat behind marching troops. This strong beat reinforces the speaker's determination.

**3.** Look at the phrase "let my feet be flippers, arms be fins." What do students think is happening here? Does the author really want to be a fish?

## Extension Activity:

Ask your students to write an "I want to" poem about something they really want to accomplish. They can also go back in time when choosing their "I want to" subject, as the poet did, and write from a memory of when they wanted badly to do something and couldn't do it. Ask them to model their writing after "I Want to Swim" and begin their phrases similarly:

I want to_____. Really_____
      Not just _____,
           but _____.

# I Want to Swim

*By Jacqueline Sweeney*

I want to swim.
Really swim.
Not just splash my
arms and legs and sink,
but swim.

I want to dive.
Really dive.
Not just smack the water
with my feet,
but dive

headfirst from
poolside,

bubbles swirling
'round my body
as I glide.

And topside, when I shake
the hair from my face
pinch the water from
my eyes,

I'll finally see the others
far behind.

Let my feet be flippers,
arms be fins.

I want to swim!

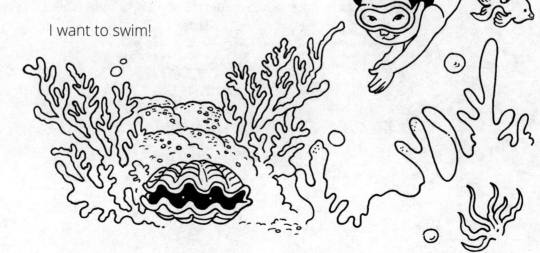

# I Want to Swim

*By Jacqueline Sweeney*

---

**PLAYERS:**   Readers 1–5

---

**Reader 1:**   "I Want to Swim" by Jacqueline Sweeney

**Reader 1:**   I want to swim. Really swim.

**Reader 2:**   Not just splash my arms and legs and sink,

**Reader 3:**   but swim.

**Reader 1:**   I want to dive. Really dive.

**Reader 2:**   Not just smack the water with my feet,

**MORE →**

**Reader 3:**     but dive

**Reader 4:**     headfirst from poolside,

**Reader 5:**     bubbles swirling 'round my body
as I glide.

**Reader 4:**     And topside,
when I shake the hair from my face,
pinch the water from my eyes,

**Reader 5:**     I'll finally see the others
far behind.

**Readers 1, 2:**     Let my feet be flippers,

**Reader 3:**     arms be fins.

**All Readers:**     I want to swim!

## Reading Tips

This poem should be read with much humor and personal expression.

Have each reader point to parts of their faces as they read.

The ending should be boisterous.

Try reading the poem as a class, with gestures, as fast as you possibly can. Challenge students to read faster. Soon, they'll be rolling with laughter!

# How to Teach "If My Face Were Outer Space"

In "If My Face Were Outer Space," the comparisons between the face and outer space keep going, going, and going. The poem uses an extended metaphor—each part of a face is reimagined with an interplanetary spin.

## Questions to ask students:

**1.** Ask students about the structure of this poem. It contains eight stanzas. The word stanza in Italian means "little room." Invite students to draw a box around each stanza. Can they see the resemblance to little rooms? Each room is different. You might point out that each stanza has four lines, which makes it a quatrain, and each quatrain has its job to do: comparing specific facial parts to objects in outer space.

**2.** Invite half of your class to refer to the text of the poem and make a list of all the outer-space nouns they can find. Have the other half make a list of all the nouns they can find that relate to the face. Bring the lists together on chart paper or the whiteboard.

**3.** You might ask if the poem has to rhyme. The answer is "no." Poems often do NOT rhyme, but in this case, the poet chose rhyme to add to the merriment and humor of the moment.

## Extension Activity:

Your students might attempt an "If I Were…" poem of their own, comparing themselves or their faces to something in nature, such as a rainforest, an ocean, a mountain, a state. Have them compose their own lists of features to use as inspiration.

# If My Face Were Outer Space

*By Jacqueline Sweeney*

If my face were outer space
My eyes would be bright moons glowing
green or brown or blue. My cheeks would be
round mountain slopes on Mars.

My nostrils would be craters. My pores
would be dwarf stars. I'd make
eyebrow explorations in small solar
powered cars.

My mouth would be a black hole
searching endlessly for food; sucking up
space objects like a vacuum cave
of doom.

I'd have galaxies of freckles
and soaring asteroid moles, and
spinning satellite pimples
orbiting my nose.

My dimples would be channels leading to
my lips and chin and the smoothest curve
of Venus where my smiles
all begin.

My hair would be like Saturn's rings
reflecting heat and light; swirling
'round my head until I go to bed
at night.

I'd have rotating space stations
floating upright as my ears, listening
in on conversations that I'm not
supposed to hear;

and I'd listen in for
years and years and
years and years and
years!

# If My Face Were Outer Space

**By Jacqueline Sweeney**

**PLAYERS:** Readers 1–7

**Reader 1:** "If My Face Were Outer Space"
by Jacqueline Sweeney

**Reader 1:** If my face were outer space,
My eyes would be bright moons glowing
green or brown or blue.
My cheeks would be round mountain slopes
on Mars.

**Reader 2:** My nostrils would be craters.
My pores would be dwarf stars.
I'd make eyebrow explorations
in small solar powered cars.

I

**MORE** ➡

**Reader 3:**     My mouth would be a black hole
searching endlessly for food;
sucking up space objects
like a vacuum cave of doom.

**Reader 4:**     I'd have galaxies of freckles
and soaring asteroid moles,
and spinning satellite pimples
orbiting my nose.

**Reader 5:**     My dimples would be channels
leading to my lips and chin
and the smoothest curve of Venus
where my smiles all begin.

**Reader 6:**     My hair would be like Saturn's rings
reflecting heat and light; swirling
'round my head until I go to bed at night.

**Reader 7:**     I'd have rotating space stations
floating upright as my ears
listening in on conversations
that I'm not supposed to hear;

**All Readers:**     and I'd listen in for
years and years
and years and years and
YEARS!